Robots in Space

Richard and Louise Spilsbury

Gareth Stevens
PUBLISHING

Please visit our website, **www.garethstevens.com**.
For a free color catalog of all our high-quality books,
call toll free 1-800-542-2595 or fax 1-877-542-2596.

Library of Congress Cataloging-in-Publication Data
Spilsbury, Richard.
Robots in space / by Richard and Louise Spilsbury.
p. cm. — (Amazing robots)
Includes index.
ISBN 978-1-4824-3013-4 (pbk.)
ISBN 978-1-4824-3016-5 (6 pack)
ISBN 978-1-4824-3014-1 (library binding)
1. Space robotics — Juvenile literature. 2. Robots — Juvenile literature.
I. Spilsbury, Richard, 1963-. II. Spilsbury, Louise. III. Title.
TL1097.S65 2016
629.43 —d23

First Edition

Published in 2016 by
Gareth Stevens Publishing
111 East 14th Street, Suite 349
New York, NY 10003

© 2016 Gareth Stevens Publishing

Produced for Gareth Stevens by Calcium
Editors for Calcium: Sarah Eason and Jennifer Sanderson
Designers: Paul Myerscough and Simon Borrough
Picture researcher: Susannah Jayes

Photo credits: Cover: Wikimedia Commons: Regan Geeseman; Inside: ESA: NASA 5t; Flickr:
NASA 34, 35, 40-41, 42, 43; NASA: 1, 5br, 9, 14, 37br, 44, JPL/University of Arizona 15, JPL-
Caltech 22, 28, JPL-Caltech/Space Science Institute 16, JPL/USGS 13; Shutterstock: Elenarts 10,
Alexander Smulskiy 7; Wikimedia Commons: Don Davis for NASA 8, NASA 4, 6, 12, 20, 21, 24,
26, 30, 33, 37t, 39, NASA Ames Research Center 45, NASA/JPL 11, 17, 25, NASA/JPL-Caltech 31,
NASA/JPL-Caltech/University of Arizona 19, NASA/JPL-Caltech/Malin Space Science Systems
29, Rtphokie 27.

Printed in the United States of America
CPSIA compliance information: Batch #CS15GS: For further information contact Gareth Stevens, New York, New York at 1-800-542-2595.

Contents

Chapter 1

Robots in Space

Space exploration is incredibly exciting. One reason people want to explore space is out of curiosity. We want to know what is out there and to find out if there could be alien life on any other planets. People also explore space to discover if there are any other planets that humans could live on in the future or that contain useful resources we could use on Earth. As the world's population grows and we run out of room in which to live or grow food, the things people discover in space might become very important.

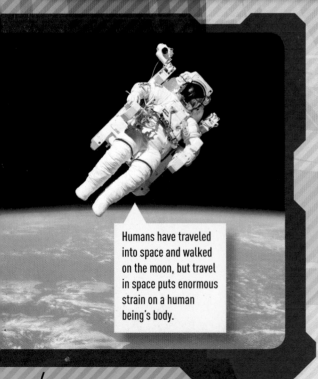

Humans have traveled into space and walked on the moon, but travel in space puts enormous strain on a human being's body.

Humans in Space

The problem with space is that it is a dangerous place for humans to be. Space has no oxygen for people to breathe and, away from the rays of the sun, temperatures plummet to -523 °F (-273 °C). It is so cold that molecules stop moving altogether! Space shuttles and space suits help protect people from the dangers of space, but even with these technologies, space travel still carries a high level of risk. Yet, without journeying into space, how can we discover more about the wonders of our universe?

This astronaut is carrying out a space walk to repair a section of the International Space Station (ISS).

Enter the Space Robot!

Space may be dangerous for humans, but it poses few threats to robots. Robotic astronauts need neither food nor drink to survive in space, and can withstand very inhospitable conditions. Very importantly, although robots are expensive to design and produce, it is far better to lose a robot in space that it is to lose a human. Both the National Aeronautics and Space Administration (NASA) and the European Space Agency (ESA) have developed robots that can travel into space alongside people. One day, these robots may be able to travel into space on their own to find out more about our galaxy, and even the realms beyond it.

Unlike human astronauts, space robots will be able to travel far beyond Earth—who knows what they may discover!

Probes

A space probe is a robotic spacecraft that is sent into space to do research. Probes travel through space to collect scientific information. There are different types of space probes because they collect different scientific information about very different environments. Probes gather pictures and data about the planets, moons, comets, and asteroids in our solar system as they fly past them. This data is important in helping to plan other space missions, such as ones to Mars and Saturn. Most probes are not designed to return to Earth, so they make a one-way journey—we could never ask astronauts to do that!

Probes are launched into space by powerful rockets.

Getting into Space

Space probes are launched into space on the back of a powerful rocket because spacecraft have to fly at very high speeds to escape the pull of Earth's gravity. Once in space, probes separate from the rocket. They then follow a course based on instructions from operators on Earth, as well as instructions that were programmed into them. With no air in space, there is no air resistance to slow them down, so the probes keep moving at high speeds. When they reach their destination, the instruments on the probes start taking measurements and sending back this information to Earth by radio. Space probes can carry special cameras, telescopes, and other instruments far out into the solar system. Many are powered by solar panels, which make electricity using energy from the sun.

The First of Many

Sputnik 1 was the first probe to go into space. It was launched on October 4, 1957, by the former Soviet Union. On January 31, 1958, the United States sent a probe called *Explorer 1* into space. Both of these probes studied Earth's upper atmosphere from space and made discoveries about what it is like to be in space. A later probe, *Explorer 6*, was launched in August 1959. It took the first pictures of Earth from orbit.

The first probe, *Sputnik 1*, was about the size of a beach ball and took 98 minutes to orbit Earth.

Robots Are the Future

In 2022, the ESA plans to launch a deep-space mission to explore the icy moons of Jupiter. The probe is called *JUICE*, which stands for Jupiter Icy Moons Explorer. It is hoped that *JUICE* will reach Jupiter by 2030. It will spend three or more years studying Jupiter's moons. Information collected by the probe will give us better insight into how gas giants and their moons form, and whether these moons could support microscopic life.

Pioneers

The *Pioneers* were Earth's first deep space probes. The first few *Pioneers* were designed to study the moon, but later versions were launched to study the outer reaches of the solar system. *Pioneer 6*, for example, sent back data about the powerful solar wind. When the solar wind reacts with Earth's magnetic field and atmosphere, it causes the beautiful displays of dancing lights in the night sky known as auroras. *Pioneer 6* was launched in 1965, and continued to send back data to Earth for 35 years, far longer than an astronaut could have survived in space!

The *Pioneers* had instruments that had never been used in space before. They were designed to study things like the components of Jupiter's atmosphere.

Pioneer 10

In December 1973, after 19 months in space, *Pioneer 10* became the first space probe to fly past Jupiter. Jupiter is more than twice as big as all of the other planets combined, and it has a system of rings and more than 60 moons. One of its moons is bigger than the planet Mercury, and three of them are larger than Earth's moon! *Pioneer 10* discovered Jupiter's magnetic tail, an extension of the planet's magnetosphere. After flying past Jupiter, *Pioneer 10* continued toward a distant star called Aldebaran. It is expected to reach that star in about 2 million years.

Pioneer 11

Launched in 1973, *Pioneer 11* flew past Jupiter in 1974. In September 1979, the probe passed within about 13,000 miles (20,922 km) of the planet Saturn. Its close-up images of Jupiter, showed some amazing features, such as a continuous giant storm known as the Great Red Spot. When *Pioneer 11* passed Saturn, it sent the first up-close photographs of the planet to scientists on Earth. It proved that the asteroid belt could be safely traversed so that later probes could venture farther into space safely. *Pioneer 10* stopped transmitting data in 2003, and communication with *Pioneer 11* was lost in 1995.

Robots Are the Future

The ESA is hoping to launch a space probe called *Don Quijote* in the near future. This space probe will carry out a mission to crash into an asteroid to see if and how the impact changes the course or direction of the asteroid. This could be useful in the future, especially if we ever need to deflect an asteroid to keep it from hitting Earth.

The *Pioneer* probes were the first to send detailed images of Jupiter and Saturn to Earth.

Voyagers 1 and 2

Pioneer 10 held the record for being the farthest human-made object in space until *Voyager 1* overtook it in 1998. *Voyager 1* and *2* are NASA robot space probes designed to observe and transmit more data about Jupiter and Saturn. However, since doing that, they have explored regions of space where no other object from Earth has gone before.

Voyager 1 travels at 35,790 miles per hour (57,600 kph). That is fast enough to travel from Earth to the sun three and a half times in one year!

How Do They Work?

Voyagers 1 and *2* are identical. Each one has equipment to carry out different experiments. These include television cameras, magnetometers for measuring magnetic forces, and sensors that can measure the heat of objects as well as detect movement. The *Voyagers* travel too far from the sun to use solar panels, so they contain devices that convert the heat produced from the natural decay of plutonium fuel on the probe into electricity. The information that the probes gather is sent by radio, and signals take about two weeks to reach Earth.

Discoveries

Voyagers 1 and *2* have traveled farther than any robots in space. One of the most amazing discoveries from *Voyager 1* was that Jupiter's moon, Io, has active volcanoes. This was the first time active volcanoes had been seen on another body in the solar system. *Voyager 2* also found a thin ring around Jupiter, making it the second planet known to have a ring, and two new moons: Thebe and Metis.

Voyager 2 is the only spacecraft that has visited Uranus and Neptune, and it is the source of a vast amount of our knowledge about those planets. In 2013, *Voyager 1* sent a sound recording to Earth as it left the solar system. This was the first time that we have ever had a recording of sounds in interstellar space. Both *Voyager* probes are still sending scientific information about their surroundings. Their current mission is to explore the outermost edge of the sun's domain and beyond.

Robots Are the Future

Each *Voyager* probe carries a gold-plated copper disc along with a cartridge, needle, and instructions explained in symbols for playing it. This is so that any aliens finding these spacecraft in the future can see and hear images and sounds that tell them about life on Earth.

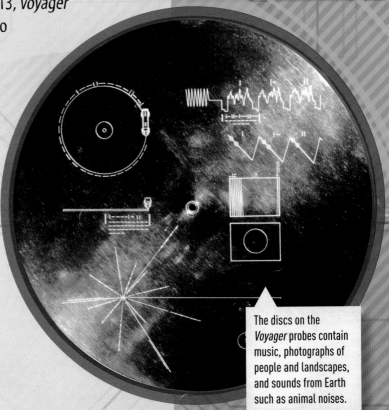

The discs on the *Voyager* probes contain music, photographs of people and landscapes, and sounds from Earth such as animal noises.

Chapter 2

Flying Around Planets

Some robot spacecraft are designed to orbit, or circle, distant planets or moons to find out more about them. Orbiters can circle many times, giving them the chance to make a detailed study of space bodies. As well as flying farther than it is possible for humans to go yet, orbiters also do a job that would be quite dull for people.

The total cost of the *Viking* project was roughly $1 billion.

Each *Viking* orbiter had eight solar panels to supply power.

Orbiters at Work

A planet exerts a gravitational pull, so a spacecraft would normally be pulled toward the planet when it got close to it. However, when a robot spacecraft is in orbit, it stays the same height above the surface of a planet, flying on a circular path around it. Orbiters can do this because they are moving so fast. The faster an object travels, the more horizontal distance it covers as it falls, and the gentler the curve of its path—so it ends up circling around and around a planet. Orbiters are usually launched and placed into orbit by rockets.

The Viking Orbiters

In 1975, within a few weeks of each other, NASA launched *Viking 1* and *2*. After completing a journey of almost a year, they entered orbits around Mars. The *Viking* orbiters were an octagon shape and measured about 8.2 feet (2.5 m) across. Each had four wings, measuring almost 32.8 feet (10 m) from tip to tip. To keep them in the correct orbit, *Viking 1* and *2* carried fuel supplies and had small rockets on top to speed them up or slow them down.

Images of Mars

The landers from the *Viking* orbiters were the first robotic spacecraft to transmit pictures from Mars's surface. They took images of almost the entire surface as they circled the planet. These images revealed things like volcanoes, giant canyons, craters, landforms created by wind, and evidence that there was once water on the Martian surface. The *Viking* orbiters also recorded weather patterns on Mars and took photographs of the planet's two tiny moons, Deimos and Phobos. Each orbiter also had a lander, or landing robotic spacecraft, which landed on the surface of Mars (see pages 18–19).

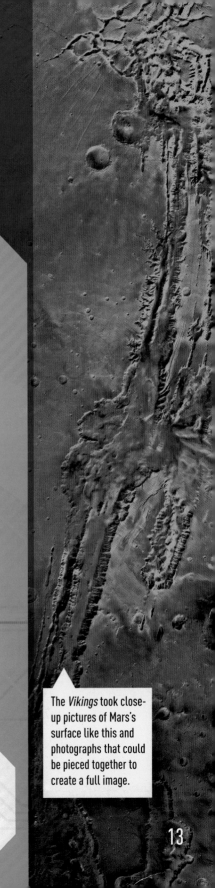

The *Vikings* took close-up pictures of Mars's surface like this and photographs that could be pieced together to create a full image.

Galileo: Studying Jupiter

In 1989, the orbiter *Galileo* was launched into space. Its task was to take photos of the planet Jupiter, as well as collecting information about its magnetic field and its moons from orbit. It took six years for *Galileo* to travel the 2.3 billion miles (3.7 billion km) to reach Jupiter's orbit, a journey that a manned spacecraft cannot do yet. So far, no rocket has been created that could take off from Earth's surface and escape its gravitational pull to reach space, while carrying the weight of a large spacecraft, astronauts, and supplies and materials needed for such a long journey.

The Space Shuttle carried the *Galileo* spacecraft in its cargo bay.

Slingshot into Space

Galileo was launched from the space shuttle *Atlantis*. It traveled to Venus and back to Earth, using the gravity of these planets to fling it, as if from a slingshot, to Jupiter. This technique is called a gravity assist. It is used to save a spacecraft time and energy. *Galileo* started working before it arrived at Jupiter, taking pictures of asteroids as it passed through the asteroid belt. It got the first close-up views of the asteroids Gaspra and Ida. At the same time, it discovered a satellite orbiting Ida.

Galileo's Mission

Just before entering Jupiter's orbit, *Galileo* released a probe that dropped slowly by parachute through part of Jupiter's atmosphere. It sent data to *Galileo* about things like the temperature and cloud structure, and measured the amount of water and other chemicals there, before the heat and pressure in the atmosphere broke through its heat shield and destroyed it.

Galileo then proceeded to fly in a series of different orbits around Jupiter, taking close-up pictures of four of the planet's moons as well as of Jupiter's clouds, auroras, and storms, including the Great Red Spot. After that, *Galileo* was sent into Jupiter's magnetic field to get closer to its innermost moon, Io, to study its active volcanoes. Jupiter's magnetic field is incredibly dangerous— it traps radiation, leading to levels that are more than 1,000 times the lethal dose for a human. The powerful radiation damaged *Galileo*. Finally, in September 2003, *Galileo* was instructed to fall into Jupiter's atmosphere and destroy itself.

Galileo took this image of a volcanic region on Io. Io gets its yellow-orange appearance from the sulfur the volcanoes give off.

Orbiters help us understand planets as a whole. They have revealed a wealth of information about Mars.

Cassini: Studying Saturn

The orbiter *Cassini* was designed to explore Saturn and its atmosphere, rings, magnetosphere, and moons. *Cassini* was launched in 1997 and reached Saturn's orbit seven years later. It was the first robotic spacecraft to orbit Saturn—*Pioneer 11* and *Voyagers 1* and *2* had only flown past.

Cassini is 22 feet (6.7 m) high and 13.1 feet (4 m) wide, which is about the same size as a 30-seater bus!

Cassini took detailed pictures of Saturn's moon, Titan.

Cassini *and* Huygens

Although NASA made the *Cassini* orbiter, it carried with it an ESA probe called *Huygens*, which measured 8.9 feet (2.7 m) across. *Cassini* released *Huygens* on December 25, 2004, and let it drop by parachute toward Titan, Saturn's largest moon. *Huygens* was equipped with six instruments, which it used to study the atmosphere and the surface of Titan. *Huygens* sent data and images back to the orbiter, which *Cassini* then transmitted to Earth.

Cassini's Discoveries

After *Cassini* released *Huygens*, it continued on to orbit Saturn numerous times and fly by the planet's other moons. *Cassini's* instruments include radar to map the cloud-covered surface of Titan, and a magnetometer to study Saturn's magnetic field. *Cassini* took amazing pictures of things like Saturn's cloud patterns, which showed that wind speeds on the planet can reach more than 1,100 miles per hour (1,770 kph)—more than four times the top speed of winds on Earth. Pictures taken by *Cassini* also showed that Saturn's moon Enceladus, which had been thought to be frozen and dead, had geysers erupting on it. This helped scientists figure out that the geysers create one of Saturn's rings. They also saw water ice in the geysers, which scientists say may mean that Enceladus has an underground ocean and even an environment possible for life. *Cassini* also discovered six new moons and two new rings around Saturn.

Robots Are the Future

In 2017, *Cassini's* orbit will be changed so that it will pass inside Saturn's innermost ring and go even nearer to Titan. After making closer orbits, *Cassini* will end its mission by plunging into Saturn. On this its final mission, it is hoped that *Cassini* will be able to tell us something about Saturn's atmosphere. before it is destroyed.

Cassini made amazing new discoveries about Saturn's rings.

Chapter 3

Other Worlds

Landers, as their name suggests, are robotic spacecraft designed to touch down on the surface of a moon, planet, or other space body. Their job is to collect images and other information about these worlds. In 1975, NASA sent two *Viking* missions to put landers on Mars: *Viking 1* and *Viking 2*. In 1976, almost a year after being launched, NASA's *Viking 1* made history when it became the first successful lander to touch down on Mars, at least 34.8 million miles (56 million km) away from Earth.

The Viking Landers

The *Viking* landers flew into space together with their orbiters, but separated and dropped to the planet's surface after entering the orbit around Mars. The dangerous thing for landers is the landing. As the landers pass through the Martian atmosphere, friction against the gases in the atmosphere causes dangerously hot temperatures of up to 3,800 °F (2,093 °C). The *Viking* landers had thick heat shields to protect them, and a parachute to slow them down a little for landing and to slightly reduce that friction. Just before landing, three lander legs with honeycomb-shaped aluminum shock absorbers were extended to soften the landing.

In 1971, the *Mars 3* lander touched down on Mars. It survived for only a few seconds and sent back no useful data.

Happy Landings

The two *Viking* landers touched down on flat areas of land about 4,000 miles (6,437 km) apart. After landing, they began taking pictures and doing scientific experiments. They analyzed the soil of Mars and took color images of its rocky surface and dusty, pinkish sky. The experiments the landers did looked for evidence of life in soil samples, but did not find any traces on the surface of the planet. Each lander went on working much longer than its planned life span of three months after touchdown. *Viking 1* made its final transmission to Earth on November 11, 1982, and the mission officially ended the following year. The mission's most amazing achievement was to send the first pictures of the surface of Mars to Earth. They showed Mars to be a cold planet with reddish volcanic soil, with some evidence of ancient riverbeds.

The *Viking* landers took 4,500 images of the surface of Mars, and more than 3 million weather-related measurements were sent back to Earth.

Pathfinder

In 1997, a new lander, *Pathfinder*, touched down about 530 miles (853 km) southeast of where *Viking 1* had landed on Mars. *Pathfinder* had been launched in December 1996 from Cape Canaveral, Florida, and using gravity assist, took only seven months to reach and land on Mars.

A New Kind of Lander

Pathfinder was a new kind of lander. It was designed to test an innovative way of landing a robotic spacecraft on a planet's surface—using air bags, not unlike the ones you find in a family automobile, to ensure a soft landing! As *Pathfinder* descended through the atmosphere on its way to the surface of Mars, it kept itself from dropping too quickly by using a parachute, a heat shield, and rockets. Just eight seconds before hitting the surface, the air bags that surrounded the lander opened, and made it look rather like a big bunch of grapes. The air bags cushioned the fall of the lander and allowed it to bounce safely several times along the surface, until finally coming to rest. In fact, *Pathfinder* was the first robotic spacecraft to bounce on another planet!

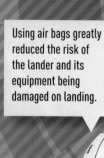

Using air bags greatly reduced the risk of the lander and its equipment being damaged on landing.

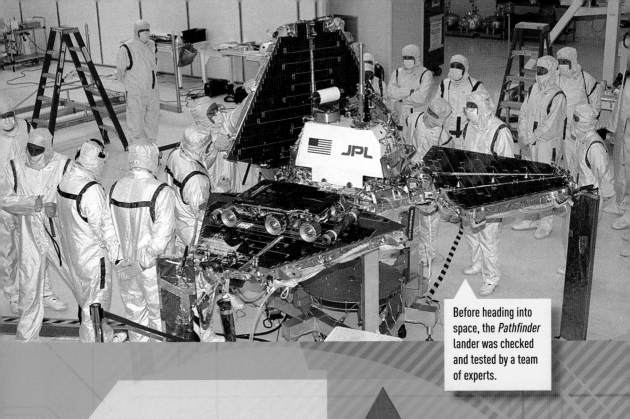

Before heading into space, the *Pathfinder* lander was checked and tested by a team of experts.

Pathfinder's Mission

Pathfinder was a tetrahedron shape, with three sides and a base, and it stood almost 3 feet (0.9 m) tall. Its main mission was to prove that a cost-effective lander could be sent to Mars, and it also sent back useful information. After landing, it unfolded to reveal the scientific instruments inside. These included magnets, thermometers, wind socks for checking the wind direction, and other equipment for investigating the atmosphere on Mars. It sent back 8.5 million different measurements and its camera system sent back more than 16,500 images that gave a vivid view of the surface of Mars. *Pathfinder* transmitted its last data on September 27, 1997.

Robots Are the Future

Over time, landers have used different methods of getting safely through the atmosphere of Mars and landing on its surface. Each time a lander goes there, designers and engineers on Earth learn more about how to make spacecraft that can do this safely. They are using this knowledge to design a spacecraft that could land people safely on Mars.

Sky Crane

In 2012, a new kind of robotic lander was invented: the *Sky Crane*. The *Sky Crane* was designed to lower a very heavy new robot, called *Curiosity* (see pages 28–29), onto Mars to move around and explore the planet's surface. *Sky Crane* was designed to land and deliver *Curiosity* safely, despite passing through the atmosphere of Mars at a potentially deadly 13,000 miles per hour (20,931 kph).

It took just seven minutes, from atmospheric entry to touchdown, for *Sky Crane* to deliver *Curiosity* onto the surface of Mars.

Ready for Action!

Sky Crane was a little like a giant, eight-rocket jetpack. As it descended toward Mars, friction with the atmosphere helped slow down Sky Crane to about 1,000 miles per hour (1,600 kph). Heat shields prevented the 3,800 °F (2,093 °C) temperatures caused by this friction from harming the Sky Crane. A parachute, 60 feet (18 m) wide, which was attached to the capsule by cables almost 160 feet (48.8 m) long, slowed the Sky Crane even more. Lower in the atmosphere, when it was safe to dump the heat shield, Sky Crane slowed to about 200 miles per hour (320 kph).

Mission Accomplished

The parachute was cut off, and Sky Crane fired its rockets to slow its descent to just 1.5 miles per hour (2.4 kph). When it got to within about 60 feet (18 m) of the surface of Mars, Sky Crane lowered Curiosity 20 feet (6 m) beneath it on three nylon ropes. It continued its slow descent until Curiosity was resting on the surface. Then the bolts holding Curiosity to the Sky Crane exploded, separating the two and leaving Curiosity to do its job. Having completed its mission, Sky Crane then flew out of reach and crashed into the surface of Mars, destroying itself.

Robots Are the Future

Could Sky Crane technology be the key to the future? Landing large spacecraft using rockets, which work by thrusting downward to force the spacecraft upward, blasts up a lot of dust from the surface, and this could damage the spacecraft. By kicking up dust and soil from the surface, the rockets could also create craters that could cause problems for vehicles as they try to land. Air bags big enough to soften a landing would be too heavy or expensive. In the future, perhaps robotic Sky Cranes could be used to land spacecraft carrying humans and their supplies on planets including Mars?

Chapter 4

Exploring the Surface

Landers can touch down on a planet's surface, but they cannot move around once they get there. This means that they can analyze or take pictures of a limited area of ground. However, the rovers that the landers carry with them and release onto the surface can move around and send back data, often via their landers. Like the orbiters and landers before them, the great advantage of the robot rovers over human astronauts is that they can "see" in wavelengths of light and energy, and feel things about magnetic fields or microscopic bits of dust that people cannot.

In 1972, during the *Apollo 17* mission, astronauts used a rover to make a short trip on the moon's surface, but rovers that go farther into space are unmanned robots.

The Sojourner Rover

The day after it landed, the *Pathfinder* lander released a six-wheeled, remote-controlled rover called *Sojourner*. *Sojourner* was 2 feet (61 cm) long, 1.5 feet (45.7 cm) wide, and 1 foot (30.5 cm) tall, and weighed around 23 pounds (10.4 kg)—about as big as an average microwave oven! It rolled down landing ramps on the side of *Pathfinder* and started its slow progress across the surface. Its maximum speed was 2 feet per minute (61 cm per minute). Solar panels and batteries powered *Sojourner*. It had two black-and-white cameras on top that took images of where it was going. *Pathfinder* also sent back images of *Sojourner's* progress, to help scientists decide where to send it. People on Earth used a computer to steer *Sojourner*. They sent instructions to *Pathfinder*, which in turn relayed them to *Sojourner*.

Sojourner was designed to travel steadily across Mars's rocky surface.

Sojourner was named by a girl who won a competition to name it. She named it after the abolitionist Sojourner Truth.

Sojourner's Mission

Over a period of two and a half months, *Sojourner* traveled 0.3 miles (0.48 km) away from *Pathfinder*. It took 550 color photographs and analyzed soil and rocks at more than 16 different sites near *Pathfinder*. Data collected by *Sojourner* and transmitted back to Earth by *Pathfinder* showed scientists that rocks on Mars were like some volcanic rocks found on Earth. These, along with information collected by robotic spacecraft, added to evidence suggesting that at some point in the past, Mars was much more like Earth than it is today, with a warmer, thicker atmosphere and water in its liquid state.

Opportunity

Opportunity is a NASA rover that was launched in 2003 and released by its lander onto the surface of Mars in January 2004. Opportunity is a six-wheeled robot equipped with a variety of instruments. These include a camera that can take close-up images of rocks, and rock-grinding tools and other equipment that analyze the rocks, soil, and dust on the surface of the planet. Its mission was designed to last 90 days, but ever since Opportunity landed in a crater, it has explored several other craters, and continues to explore today.

Opportunity weighs 384 pounds (174.2 kg). It measures 5.2 feet (1.6 m) long and is 4.9 feet (1.5 m) high.

Mars Roving

Like *Sojourner*, *Opportunity* is sent instructions about where to move from the Jet Propulsion Laboratory (JPL). The JPL is the NASA command control center and is about 125 million miles (200 million km) away from Mars here on Earth. *Opportunity's* six large wheels have thick treads to provide grip when it moves over slopes and rocks, and to prevent it slipping on sand as it climbs in and out of craters. Each wheel also has its own motor to move the rover in all directions. *Opportunity* runs on solar power, but it does not need a lot of energy because the thin atmosphere on Mars offers far less air resistance than there is on Earth. This means that the rover does not have to accelerate much to move. *Opportunity* also has a suspension system to help it avoid tipping over. The wheels are connected to the rover body in a way that absorbs some of the impact when the rover hits a bump.

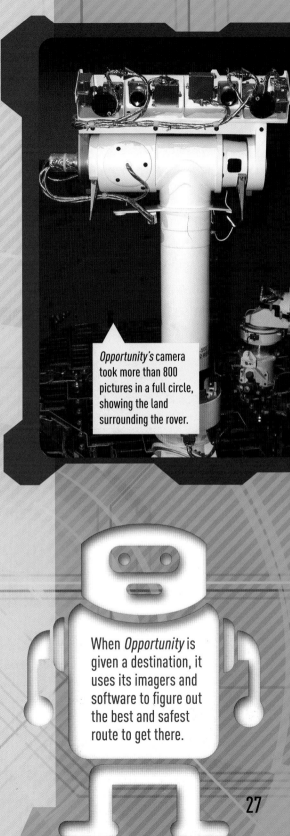

Opportunity's camera took more than 800 pictures in a full circle, showing the land surrounding the rover.

Setbacks and Successes

Despite a few problems—*Opportunity* was stuck in a sand dune and dust storms threatened to clog its solar panels—this rover has traveled more than 25 miles (40.2 km) on Mars, setting a new off-Earth driving record. It has also made some interesting discoveries. For example, it found evidence of past water and rocks that may have been part of the shoreline of an ancient body of salty water.

When *Opportunity* is given a destination, it uses its imagers and software to figure out the best and safest route to get there.

27

Curiosity

The *Curiosity* rover, which was lowered onto the surface of Mars by the *Sky Crane*, is about 9 feet (2.7 m) long. It weighs about 2,000 pounds (907.2 kg), which is about four times as heavy as *Opportunity*. *Curiosity* cost $2.5 billion to build and it is the longest, heaviest rover on Mars. It is capable of exploring a far greater area than any Mars rover before it. *Curiosity* is equipped like a mobile science laboratory, so it can find out if living things were ever able to live on the planet or if they ever could. It was launched by rocket from Cape Canaveral, in November 2011, and it landed in the Gale Crater on Mars in August 2012.

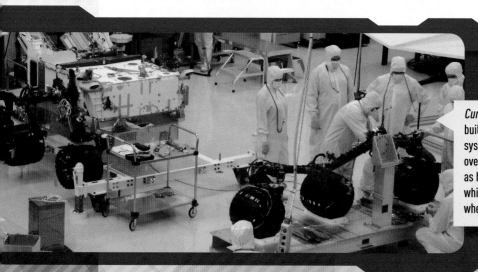

Curiosity's engineers built its suspension system so it can climb over obstacles twice as high as its wheels, while keeping all six wheels on the ground.

Curiosity Stats and Facts

It takes about 90 people, based at the JPL, to operate a Mars rover. *Curiosity* generates its power using heat from the natural decay of plutonium. Its wheels have a diameter of 20 inches (50.8 cm) and its robotic arm is 7 feet (2.1 m) long. Its suspension system helps it roll over rocks and other obstacles up to 29 inches (73.7 cm) high and to travel an average of 98 feet per hour (30 m/h).

Discoveries

The *Curiosity* rover can travel up to 12 miles (19.3 km) and has used its instruments to study rocks and soils to see what it was like on Mars in the past. *Curiosity* has made several important discoveries. In September 2012, it took pictures of gravel that had been eroded by water, suggesting that Gale Crater was probably once the site of an ancient stream. It also found that in the past, Mars could have had an atmosphere that supported life. However, it found no evidence of methane in the air (methane gas is a sign of life) and it found radiation levels that could pose health risks to astronauts.

Robots Are the Future

Curiosity has shown that we can safely land a very heavy, large robotic spacecraft on the surface of Mars and at a fairly specific site. Scientists believe that in the near future, a rover might be able to do a return mission and bring back rocks and soils to Earth. This would allow scientists to study them in a laboratory.

In October 2012, *Curiosity* took 55 "selfies," which were pieced together to create this full-color image of the rover on Mars.

Studying Mars

Scientists are especially interested in Mars because it is the planet that most resembles our own. It has a solid, rocky surface, and seasons and days as long as those on Earth. Although it is very cold, it would be more hospitable than a planet like Venus, which is burning hot and has a poisonous atmosphere

The rovers that study Mars are equipped like mobile science labs with a geology toolbox!

Traveling to Mars

Human travel to Mars is impossible today because a rocket big enough to carry all the fuel and supplies needed for the journey would not be able to take off. However, discoveries made by rovers and other robotic spacecraft could help us find ways of traveling and living there in the future. To study Mars, the rovers we send there have a variety of different tools and equipment.

Rover Tools

Rovers are designed to look for and find interesting rocks and soils, and then to move to those areas and study them. They have a robotic arm that holds and adjusts several instruments. The arm can reach toward a rock, and use a hand-like structure at the end of the arm, which is shaped like a cross, to hold different tools at different angles. These tools include:

▶ A spectrometer. Many of the rocks on Mars contain the metal iron so there is a lot of iron in the soil, too. This device tests exactly how much and what type of iron is in a sample.

▶ A rock abrasion tool. This grinder can drill a hole about 2 inches (5 cm) in diameter and 0.2 inches (5 mm) deep into rock to get samples for analysis.

▶ A microscopic imager. This is a microscope and a camera that takes close-up and very detailed pictures of rocks and soils.

▶ An APX spectrometer. This analyzes the chemicals that make up rocks and soils using x-rays.

Curiosity has a camera on top of a mast on its head that is made up of two "eyes" (lenses). This camera can take color pictures but also has filters that analyze rocks to help scientists decide whether or not to send the rover to check out those samples.

Robots Are the Future

One reason scientists study how much iron there is in surface rocks on Mars is because they believe that one day, they might be able to send up machines to extract rock containing iron. They could then turn this iron ore into iron metal that could be used to build machines, shelters, and other structures that people need.

Chapter 5

Robotic Arms

Rovers rely on robotic arms to carry equipment, for example, to take samples or to see where they are going. On Earth, robotic arms are used for a wide range of purposes. Some arms spray-paint or weld pieces of metal together to make new cars. Others are used by surgeons to perform delicate operations or by soldiers to detect and explode bombs or mines. Whatever their use, and whatever tools they carry, most arms work in similar ways.

What Is a Robotic Arm?

A robotic arm is made up of several parts, rather like a human arm. It has several long, stiff pieces or links, like our long bones. These are connected and moved relative to each other by joints that are usually rotary joints, like our shoulder joints. There are other types of joints, too, such as joints that slide two long pieces together or apart in the same direction. Each joint is powered by an electric motor. This provides the force to rotate or extend the links to or from each other. Our arms move our hands to the position where they need to work or do something, such as feed us or operate a joystick. The wrist joint and finger joints then operate the hand. This is the same in robotic arms, where the arm is called a manipulator because it positions the "hand," or end effector. The end effector's job is to position and operate a variety of tools connected to the "wrist" joint.

Space Crane

One of the simplest arms in space is found on the Russian part of the ISS. Called the Strela Crane, this telescopic pole can extend up to 46 feet (14 m) and is attached by a rotary joint. It is used to move large, bulky objects from one place to another on the ISS, like unloading cargo from spacecraft. Unlike arms in use in space today, the Strela is not powered. It has to be extended or shortened using a hand crank, which is tiring for astronauts. However, as there is no need to plug in the arm, it can be located anywhere on the ISS using a second Strela.

The ISS Strela Cranes are operated by spacewalkers outside the station, rather than from a console inside the ISS.

The Strela Cranes are used to move astronauts and components around the outside of the ISS.

33

Canadarm

In November 1981, the second ever space shuttle mission, STS-2, took the robotic arm known as Canadarm into space for the first time. It soon became the workhorse of the shuttle program and was used right up to final shuttle mission in 2011.

Jobs for Canadarm

Canadarm had two shoulder joints, one elbow joint, and three wrist joints. It had a grabber end effector. The arm could stretch out to 50 feet (15 m) long, and by gripping a metal beam, it could reach even farther so astronauts could inspect and mend damage at any point on the shuttle. Canadarm not only shifted cargo but could also hold up astronauts away from the shuttle, for example, to mend objects, such as the Hubble Space Telescope. The arm was fixed into the shuttle's hold and could unfold once the payload doors were opened.

Canadarm is a remote-controlled mechanical arm that can bend and turn with more flexibility than even a human arm!

Canadarm's Vital Stats

The arm was hollow and weighed 900 pounds (408.2 kg) on Earth. Although it could not support its own weight on Earth, it could do that and lift more than 586,000 pounds (265,805 kg) in the microgravity conditions in space. Heavy objects carried by the shuttle were usually large and could damage the shuttle, especially when being unloaded from the cargo bay. Astronauts trained for many hours on Earth to learn how to control the sensitive joystick that moved Canadarm. It was accurate enough to put a peg in a hole with fewer than 0.1 inches (0.2 cm) clearance. This accuracy proved very useful, for example, to knock ice from a shuttle vent that was clogged with frozen wastewater.

Improved Canadarm

Engineers have built a new and improved Canadarm to work on the ISS. Today's Canadarm2 is a longer, heavier version of the Canadarm that was first used on the ISS in 2001. Its greater power gives it the ability not only to help visiting spacecraft to dock, but also to unload components and assemble them into new parts of the ISS. Unlike the original Canadarm, Canadarm2 can move around! There are several ports around the ISS that either end of the arm can plug itself into to get power and link to the controller. Another improvement is that Canadarm2 can walk much like a looping caterpillar by connecting a free end to the next port, then releasing the fixed end from its starting port, and so on.

Canadarm is used to deploy, capture and repair satellites, position astronauts, and move cargo.

Dextre: Space Oddjobber

In 2008, a new robot started work on the ISS. Dextre's job was to perform a range of routine tasks that normally would have to be done by astronauts on spacewalks. Getting a robot to do the work frees up time for the astronauts, giving them a chance to stay on the ISS to conduct experiments. There are many typical chores for Dextre. These include replacing the dead batteries used to store power on the ISS, opening and closing covers, connecting cables, and changing fuses. Occasional tasks in its job description include helping to carry out scientific experiments and testing new tools.

Dextre is operated by controllers at NASA's Johnson Space Center and the Canadian Space Agency in Quebec.

All in a Day's Work

Dextre is a robot hand much bigger than a person. It has two arms measuring more than 12 feet (3.7 m) long, each with seven joints. The arms can move side to side, down and up, rotate, and bend backward. Each joint is sealed to prevent grease floating off into space. Each arm is tipped with an end effector like a multi-tool. It contains a powered socket wrench, camera, and lights for astronauts on ISS to see what it is doing, and a plug-in power connector. There are also sensors so that it can detect how much force to use, for example in moving accurately to a particular position, in gripping an object, or in tightening up bolts without breaking them. Dextre can move on the spot so it can work all around where it is located.

This picture of Dextre, also known as the Special Purpose Dextrous Manipulator (SPDM), was taken by a crew member on the ISS.

Space Railroad

Canadarm2 and Dextre are part of a mobile servicing system on the ISS. A third robot completes the system. This is a movable base to which the two arms attach, which can slide on rails from one end of the ISS to the other. This base can support both arms, plus the weights they are carrying, and move them more quickly and easily around the station on the space railroad. The base can also transport astronauts and their tools. It has inbuilt cameras to view the exterior of the ISS and the arms in action.

Dextre can ride on the end of Canadarm2 or on the Mobile Base System to move from work site to work site.

Chapter 6

Robonaut: Astronaut of the Future

On the ISS, Robonaut (a robotic astronaut), is helping human astronauts with their work. Robonaut is a new kind of robot. It is not just a useful machine that can do work usually done by humans—it looks a little like a human, too! It is the size of a human in a spacesuit and it has a head, body, arms, and hands. Its head has cameras that work a little like human eyes!

Robot Hands

Robonaut is designed to do tasks that could normally be done only by humans, not robots. To do this it needs to be able to use "hands" to do work. The challenge for the robotics development team was to build a machine with the amazing levels of dexterity, movement, and strength of a human being. With Robonaut, they achieved this. Robonaut's hands move like human hands and, with the help of the ISS team, Robonaut posted its first social media message via a smartphone on July 26, 2010!

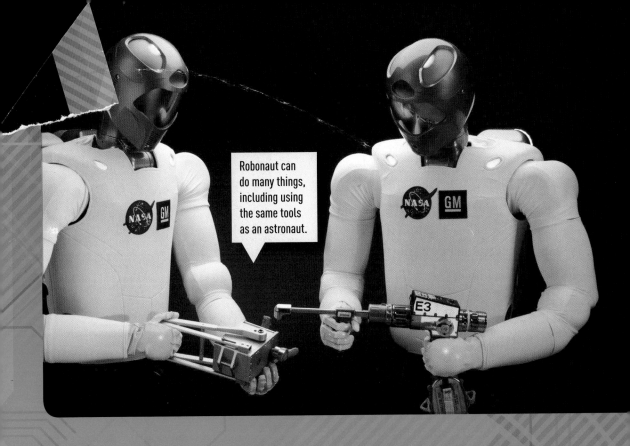

Robonaut can do many things, including using the same tools as an astronaut.

Useful R2

Robonaut 1 was built and designed at NASA's Johnson Space Center in Houston, Texas. It was tested in the laboratory but never left the ground. Robonaut 2, also known as R2, was an improved version and in 2011, the space shuttle Discovery launched this robot's head, upper body, and arms to the ISS. At first, R2 did not really do anything useful. It simply took part in a number of experiments to check its ability to push buttons, flip switches, and use tools that human astronauts normally operate. However, R2 learns as it does things, and it is becoming more and more useful!

Robots Are the Future

Robonaut is currently used only inside the ISS, but NASA hopes that Robonaut will one day be tested outside the Station. If tests are successful, a robot astronaut may even journey to planets beyond our own solar system in the future.

Robonaut in Action

At the moment, Robonaut is using its capabilities to do dull, repetitive tasks on the ISS, which is a common use for robots everywhere. For example, it acts as a cleaner, wiping down surfaces, and cleaning handrails, as well as doing other boring tasks such as monitoring air flow from vents. In 2014, after months of being tested on the ground, a pair of legs was launched to the ISS and attached to R2 in August that same year. The next stage is for Robonaut to learn to use these legs and for astronauts to test Robonaut to see how useful it can be in space. Its amazing legs are just one part of the Robonaut's body that make this robot so special.

The neck can turn and bend so that Robonaut can look up, down, left, and right.

The backpack holds R2's power system.

There is no room in its head for a "brain," so the robot's powerful computer processors are housed in its stomach.

Robonaut has used sign language to say hello to the world. It was also the first humanoid to shake hands in space!

R2's legs are not like human legs. They have seven joints to make them very flexible. They can stretch out to a length of 9 feet (2.7 m). Instead of feet they have clamping devices that can grip handrails and other objects, leaving R2's hands free to do work. There are cameras in the feet, so it will be able to "see" where it is going.

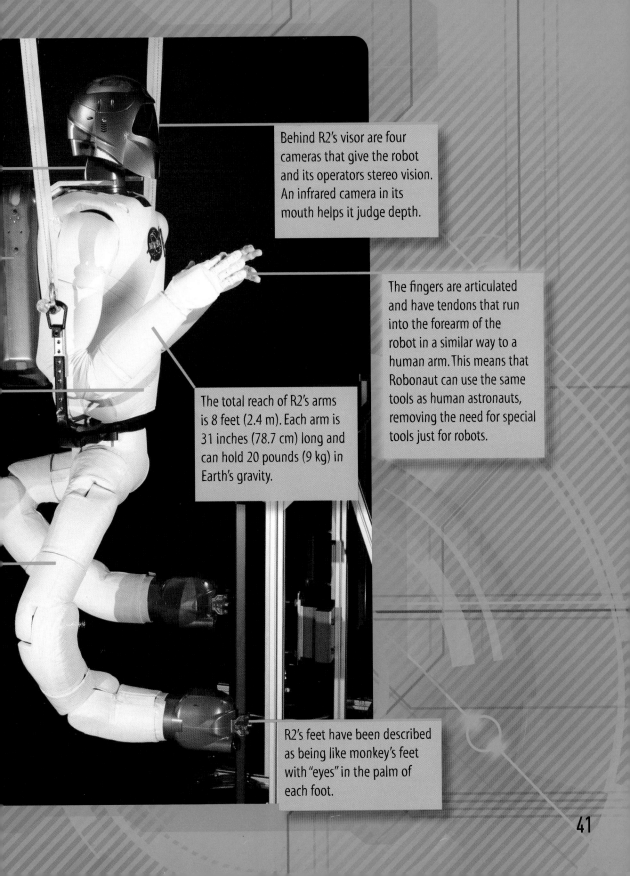

Behind R2's visor are four cameras that give the robot and its operators stereo vision. An infrared camera in its mouth helps it judge depth.

The fingers are articulated and have tendons that run into the forearm of the robot in a similar way to a human arm. This means that Robonaut can use the same tools as human astronauts, removing the need for special tools just for robots.

The total reach of R2's arms is 8 feet (2.4 m). Each arm is 31 inches (78.7 cm) long and can hold 20 pounds (9 kg) in Earth's gravity.

R2's feet have been described as being like monkey's feet with "eyes" in the palm of each foot.

Controlling Robonaut

Robonaut performs its functions in two ways. It comes loaded with a set of commands that tell it how to do certain tasks by itself. An operator keeps an eye on what it is doing so that corrections can be made while R2 is working. Robonaut can also be remote-controlled, either by an astronaut on the ISS or by an operator at mission control on Earth.

Copy-Cat Robonaut

The person who controls R2 from the ground wears a virtual-reality face helmet and gloves. The helmet is remotely linked to the robot's head, so the operator can see what the robot sees. When the operator moves his or her head and neck, R2 does the same. The gloves are remotely linked to R2's hands. When the operator wants R2 to pick up something, he or she uses its cameras to find and identify the object, then reaches out and grabs it, which makes the robot reach for it, too. One of the problems with controlling R2 from far away is that signals take time to transmit over long distances. Signals between Earth and the ISS take a couple of seconds to get there, and sometimes they cut out completely. Astronauts on the ISS control R2 through keyboard commands on a laptop. One astronaut even managed to make R2 catch a floating roll of tape inside a laboratory on the ISS.

Engineers work closely with Robonauts to improve their skills.

42

Robonaut's operators see what Robonaut sees on live video from the head cameras behind its helmet.

A Careful Worker

ISS operators on the ground and astronauts on the Space Station have been testing R2's dexterity by making the robot work with flexible things like space blankets. When the robot touches an object, tiny sensors on its fingers measure the amount of force being used. This helps Robonaut do delicate jobs that most robots, which have to be perfectly lined up next to a target to do their job, cannot do. Robonaut can feel its way on a job, checking, for example, that a peg is lined up properly in a hole, move the peg slightly until it is, and then hammer it into place.

Robots Are the Future

At the moment Robonaut can be powered only through an extension cord connected to the ISS's electrical supply. A power backpack is being developed and tested so that Robonaut will soon be able move longer distances and roam outside the ISS on its own.

Space Robots of the Future

In the future, R2 will be able to move around outside the ISS and other spacecraft. Astronauts go on spacewalks like this to set up science experiments, make repairs, or test new equipment. They also do spacewalks to extend the ISS. Humans can go outside a spacecraft for a limited time only, and they may not always be able to cope in an emergency. R2 will be able to stay out much longer as it does not need to break for lunch or sleep. It can also respond to emergencies.

Other Robonauts

Robonaut 2 is not the only robonaut. There are four others, and more in the development stages. In the future, these robonauts could be fitted with wheels or jetpacks. Robonauts with wheels would be able to drive across the moon and Mars, and robonauts with jetpacks could explore space. Another major innovation for the future is to train robonauts to be medics, nurses, and doctors, who can perform routine and life-saving operations. NASA is training a robonaut to do medical tasks like finding a pulse and giving an injection.

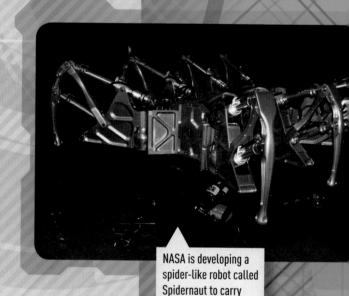

NASA is developing a spider-like robot called Spidernaut to carry increasingly heavy loads across uneven planet surfaces.

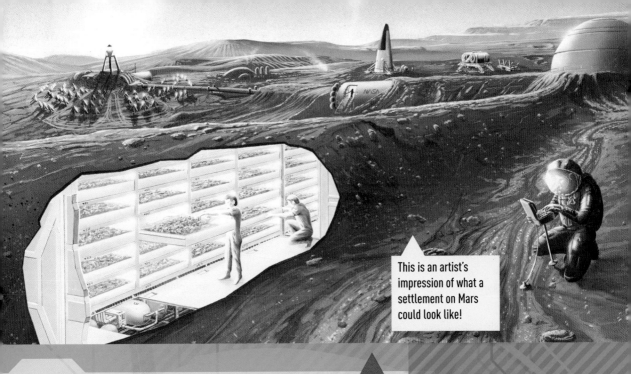

This is an artist's impression of what a settlement on Mars could look like!

How Robots Help

Creating robots that work in space does not only help us learn more about the world beyond our own planet, but it also means people can use the technology to create humanoid robots to help us with tasks on Earth. As robonauts develop the skills to work in places that would be too dangerous for humans in space, they could also be used to help us in unsafe places on Earth, such as near volcanoes or in nuclear power stations. Technologies developed for robonauts could also be used to improve or make new robots for the armed forces or factories, or for underwater exploration. Robots created to heal astronauts in space could also be used to treat people here on Earth!

Robots Are the Future

In spite of the advantages of using robots in space, some people question whether they could ever replace humans. They say that although astronaut missions are more dangerous and expensive than robot missions, robots will do only what they are programmed to do, while people will notice things that were previously unknown. What do you think?

Glossary

accelerate speed up

air resistance the force that slows down the movement of an object through the air

alien a being from another world

articulated having two or more sections connected by a flexible joint

asteroid belt the band of asteroids between the orbits of Mars and Jupiter

asteroids small rocky bodies found in space

atmosphere the layer of different gases that surrounds a planet or moon

auroras patterns of colorful, dancing lights in a planet's atmosphere

comets objects in space that have long, bright tails when they pass near the sun

craters large dips in a planet's surface, caused by the impact of another object

dexterity the ability to use hands skillfully

eroded worn away and carried somewhere new by wind or other forms of weather

filters devices that allow only some kinds of light to pass through them

friction when one thing rubs against the surface of another and creates some heat

galaxy one of the very large groups of stars that make up the universe

gas giants the four large planets that are made mainly from gases. They are Uranus, Jupiter, Neptune, and Saturn

geology the study of rocks and soil

geysers holes in the surface that shoot out water vapor and ice particles

gravity the force of attraction between two objects

gravity assist when a spacecraft uses the gravity of a planet to speed up, slow down, or change direction

Hubble Space Telescope a space telescope in orbit around Earth

infrared rays of light that cannot be seen

interstellar outside the solar system, among the distant stars

joints places where two things or parts, such as bones, are joined

magnetic field the area where the magnetic force of an object such as a planet can be felt

magnetosphere the region around a planet where the planet's magnetic field dominates

microgravity very weak gravity

molecule the smallest possible amount of a particular substance that has all the characteristics of that substance

orbit the path one object in space takes around another

oxygen a gas in the air that living things need to breathe but which also burns fuels to release heat and other gases

plutonium a radioactive substance that is used to make nuclear energy

radar a device that sends out radio waves for finding out the position and speed of a moving object

radiation a type of dangerous and powerful energy

remote control operating a machine from a distance

resources supplies of something useful, such as air, water, or fuel

satellite an electronic device placed in orbit around Earth. Weather satellites are used to collect weather information

sensors devices that sense things such as heat or movement

shock absorbers devices that reduce the effect of traveling over a bumpy surface

solar panels panels that use the energy in sunlight to make electricity

solar system the sun and the planets, and other objects that move around it

solar wind the electrically and magnetically charged particles sent out from the sun

space shuttles reusable spacecraft that can carry people and cargo between Earth and space

spacewalk when an astronaut gets out of the spacecraft while it is in space

suspension system the parts of a vehicle that help it absorb the shock of bumps as it drives across rough ground

telescopes devices that help people see things that are far away

tendons parts that connect a muscle to a bone in the human body

tetrahedron a flat-sided solid object with four faces

thrusting pushing with a lot of force

virtual reality an artificial world created by a computer that is controlled by the person who is experiencing it

wavelengths rays of light that travel at different speeds

x-rays invisible rays of light that can pass through objects to see inside them

For More Information

Books

Kops, Deborah. *Exploring Space Robots* (Searchlight Books TM—What's Amazing about Space?). Minneapolis, MN: Lerner Publications, 2013.

Owen, Ruth. *Probes* (Objects in Space). New York, NY: Powerkids Press, 2015.

Pocket Genius: Space. New York, NY: DK Children, 2012.

Shulman, Mark. *TIME For Kids Explorers: Robots.* New York, NY: Time For Kids, 2014.

Websites

Find out more about space by logging on to the NASA site at:
http://starchild.gsfc.nasa.gov/docs/StarChild/StarChild.html

Learn more about space robots at:
www.learnaboutrobots.com/space.htm

NASA has a site about space robotics at:
www.nasa.gov/education/robotics

Publisher's note to educators and parents: Our editors have carefully reviewed these websites to ensure that they are suitable for students. Many websites change frequently, however, and we cannot guarantee that a site's future contents will continue to meet our high standards of quality and educational value. Be advised that students should be closely supervised whenever they access the Internet.

Index

LiTTLe CLouD

The Science of a Hurricane

Johanna Wagstaffe

Julie McLaughlin

ORCA BOOK PUBLISHERS

Let me tell you a story about a little cloud
that wanted to become a hurricane.

cumulu[s]

nimbostratus

↑ stratus

cumulonimbus

cirrus

altostratus

altocumulus

This little cloud was born just off the west coast of Africa.

condensation
warm water makes clouds

evaporation
Water warmed by the sun goes

Weather Fact

Clouds are made up of billions of little water droplets floating in the sky. The droplets are so small you can't see them. Some clouds are high in the sky, and some are closer to the ground. They come in all shapes and sizes. Clouds get their names on the basis of where they are in the sky and what they look like.

precipitation

the clouds move over land and cool down, causing rain to fall

runoff

rainwater falls into rivers and runs back into the ocean to start the cycle again!

groundwater

Weather Fact

Like clouds, hurricanes are part of the water cycle. Hurricanes need warm water to grow, so they usually start in tropical places.

Carried by the breeze, the little cloud continued to drift west toward North America. As it moved over warmer water, it started to get stronger and bigger.

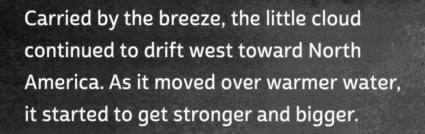

I'm a cumulus

Weather Fact

Hurricanes are steered by the winds around them—like the sails on a ship. Those winds can be so strong that they are able to take a hurricane across an ocean.

Weather Fact

Did you know that hurricanes, typhoons and cyclones are all the same kind of storm? They start as clusters of thunderstorms that begin to rotate over tropical waters and are called *tropical cyclones*. What they're eventually called is determined by where in the world they form. Our little cloud will first get classified as a tropical disturbance, then be given a number as he becomes a tropical depression. Next step is tropical storm, and then finally, because he formed in the Atlantic Ocean, he will be called a hurricane. And there are different categories of hurricane strength too.

That strength changed the little cloud. It wasn't just a little cloud anymore. It became a little storm called a tropical depression.

HURRICANE CATEGORIES

CATEGORY 1
74-95 mph winds (120-153 kmh)

It's windy, but most homes won't be damaged.

CATEGORY 2
96-110 mph winds (154-177 kmh)

Getting stronger! Some windows and roofs will see damage.

CATEGORY 3
111–130 mph winds (179–209 kmh)

It's really windy now!
Most homes will see damage.

CATEGORY 4

131–155 mph winds (211–249 kmh)

The wind is so strong now that very
few homes will be able to stay put.

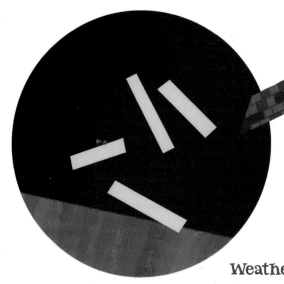

CATEGORY 5

Winds greater than 155 mph (250 kmh)

It's too windy now for homes to stay strong.
Many will be completely destroyed.

Weather Fact

Scientists give storms special names on the basis of the speed of their winds.
Not just any storm gets to be a hurricane. The winds have to be moving at
74 miles (120 kilometers) per hour to be labeled a hurricane. The strongest
hurricane winds travel at more than 186 miles (300 kilometers) per hour.

As the tropical depression moved along, it got even stronger and changed again, becoming a tropical storm. Something very special happened to the little storm then. Scientists gave it a name—Nate. The little storm had always wanted a name.

Weather Fact

Every strong tropical cyclone gets its own name. That's important, because there can be more than one storm in the world at the same time. It avoids confusion when scientists are warning people about a storm coming their way. Imagine if everyone in your class had the same name!

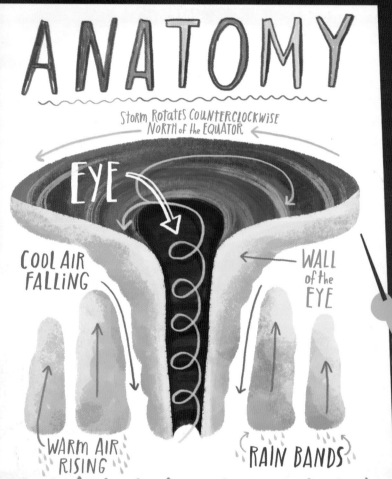

Finally Nate's winds were strong enough that he became a full hurricane! He loved his spinning winds and towering clouds, but his favorite part was his eye.

Weather Fact

The eye of a hurricane is the center of the storm. It's very calm there—blue sky, birds chirping. The rest of the storm spins around the eye. The strongest winds are beside the eye.

As Nate moved across the water, he saw something in the distance—he was getting closer to land. And to all the people and their homes on that land. The people were already talking about Nate and getting ready for his arrival.

Weather Fact

Scientists try to predict when and where a hurricane will reach land and how strong the winds will be. Scientists and officials issue a series of weather warnings before the storm arrives to help people prepare and stay safe.

ALERT!! HURRICANE WARNING!

Weather Fact

There are things that can make a hurricane lose its strength. Moving over cold water will take away its energy. Very strong winds at the top of the hurricane can tear the storm apart. A hurricane weakens as it travels over land, away from its warm-water fuel. Mountains are a hurricane's worst enemy because they do both—they take away the warm water and tear the storm apart.

They were hoping that Nate would miss them...

...but just in case, they prepared for Nate. Nate couldn't slow down or change course on his own, but he didn't want to scare the people down below!

Weather Fact

Scientists are able to make predictions about hurricanes several days in advance. Their forecast gets better as the storm gets closer. They look at satellite pictures of the storm from space and measure temperature and winds, using instruments attached to buoys or to balloons high up in the sky. There are even special planes that can fly right into the storm.

Scientists then tell emergency officials what to expect so they can start preparing people. Sometimes this means telling people to stock up on water and supplies in case the power goes out. Or it could mean canceling events so that people stay indoors. Sometimes it means asking people to leave their homes and go somewhere safer.

The job of reporters is to make sure everyone is getting the right message.

As Nate got closer to the land, he realized he would roll over the tall mountains along the coast as he made landfall. And as he moved away from the warm water, he began to weaken. He could feel the tops of the mountains starting to slow him down.

Weather Fact

A slow hurricane might sound like a good thing. But slow refers to how fast the storm is moving forward, not how strong its winds are. Slow storms are the most dangerous kind because they bring strong winds and rain to one area for a long time. If a hurricane hits a mountain and slows down over the peaks, communities on the other side will be spared the worst of the storm.

Nate slowed down so much, in fact, that he almost stopped. All the warm air that had churned inside him and given him strength turned into raindrops that flowed out of him.

Weather Fact

Hurricanes are known for their heavy rain and strong winds. These winds act like a bulldozer, pushing ocean water ahead of the storm. When this mound of water gets to the coastline, it can create dangerous flooding called *storm surge*. Even the very edges of a spinning hurricane can create thunderstorms and tornadoes!

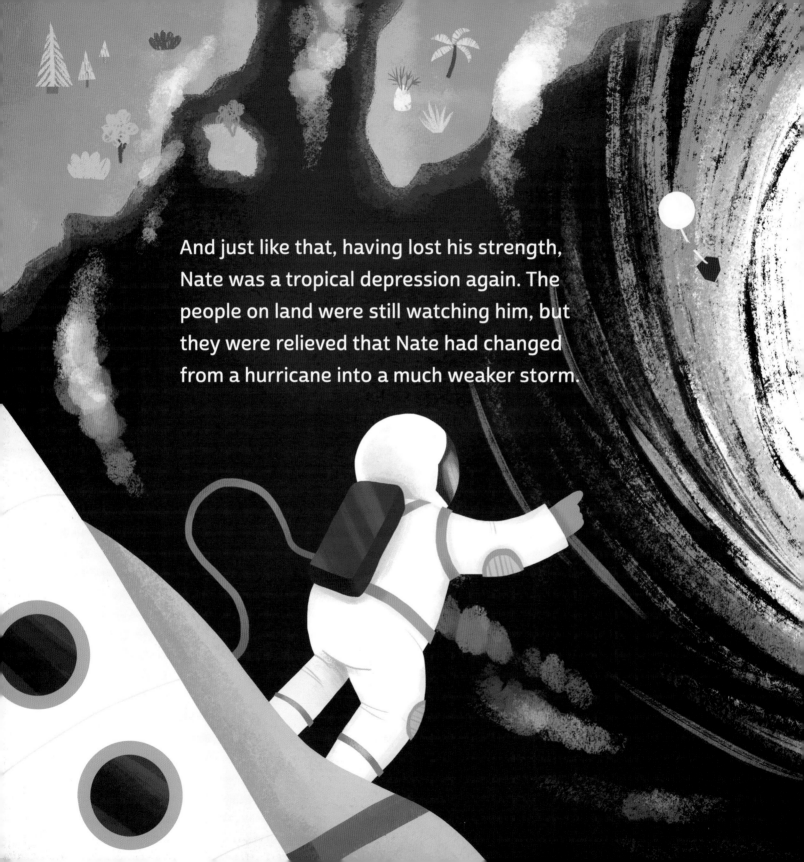

And just like that, having lost his strength, Nate was a tropical depression again. The people on land were still watching him, but they were relieved that Nate had changed from a hurricane into a much weaker storm.

Weather Fact

As technology improves, forecasters will make better hurricane predictions. New satellites going into space will help track storms with more accuracy than ever before. Computers are getting faster and more powerful at correctly determining what directions storms might take.

Even though he never made it to land as a hurricane, the little cloud still managed to cause a lot of problems. As he drifted northward and became just a few water droplets once again, the little cloud wondered what his next adventure would be and hoped that, whatever it was, he could bring some good weather to people instead.

Weather Fact

Did you know that every drop of water on our planet has been recycling itself for four billion years?

FACT PAGE

- The World Meteorological Organization assigns names to storms. It creates a list of names, starting with the letter *A* and continuing through to the letter *Z*, for each of six years and then rotates them. But if a certain hurricane is really destructive, its name will be retired forever. Until 1978, hurricanes had only female names, such as Carol, Hazel and Edna. Now names are male and female.

- Did you know that storms north of the equator rotate counterclockwise and storms south of the equator rotate clockwise? That's because of how the earth rotates.

- The east coast of North America usually gets about seven hurricanes every four years.

- One of the most well-known hurricanes is Hurricane Katrina, which killed more than 1,800 people in the United States and caused more than $150 billion in damage. The city of New Orleans was hit particularly hard—80 percent of the city was flooded.

- Because hurricanes need warm water to form, there is an official beginning and end to a hurricane season. In the Atlantic Ocean the season runs from about June 1 to November 30. For the waters around North and Central America, the season officially begins on May 15 and ends November 30. Of course, storms can form before or after the usual time frame.

- Humans are changing the climate of the planet. Because temperatures are increasing, ice is melting and oceans are rising. This means higher storm surge, more rain and more fuel for our hurricanes. So scientists need your help to learn as much as you can about the world around you. The more understanding you have about storms, the more changes you can make. Who knows, maybe you'll even help save an entire city from a hurricane one day!

Johanna

ALERT!! HURRICANE WARNING!

AUTHOR'S NOTE

Hurricanes, tornadoes, flooding, blizzards—the list goes on. Severe weather can be a fascinating force of nature. In fact, my favorite classes when I was a student were the ones about destructive weather. How can the skies that give us the perfect beach day or a magical winter morning be the same skies that create a hurricane with winds so strong they can knock down trees?

It was this curiosity that started me off on my journey to become a *meteorologist.* I use science to figure out what the weather will be like before you head out for the day. And I also forecast severe weather—like hurricanes—that might be dangerous to a lot of people.

In 2018 I was sent to Florida to report on a hurricane for the first time. Hurricane Irma was a category 5 storm, and it looked like it was headed straight for the east coast. It was scary to feel the winds picking up in strength. We were evacuated from our hotel because of the approaching storm. In the end we were spared the worst of it, but I experienced hurricane winds so strong I could barely stand. Luckily, I had a whole team helping to keep me safe so that I could tell people where the worst winds would be.

Just like Nate, I would rather have good weather to tell people about, but I like knowing I can help people stay safe.

To my own little cloud and all the adventures that lie ahead.
—J.W.

For my family, my partner and my furricane, Mr. Pants.
—J.M.

Text copyright © Johanna Wagstaffe 2020
Illustrations copyright © Julie McLaughlin 2020

Cataloguing in Publication information available from Library and Archives Canada

Issued in print and electronic formats.
ISBN 9781459821842 (hardcover) | ISBN 9781459821859 (PDF) |
ISBN 9781459821866 (EPUB)

Library of Congress Control Number: 2019943960
Simultaneously published in Canada and the United States in 2020

Summary: This STEM-based picture book describes the origin of a hurricane, telling the story of a little cloud that becomes a life-threatening storm.

Orca Book Publishers is committed to reducing the consumption of nonrenewable resources in the making of our books. We make every effort to use materials that support a sustainable future.

Orca Book Publishers gratefully acknowledges the support for its publishing programs provided by the following agencies: the Government of Canada, the Canada Council for the Arts and the Province of British Columbia through the BC Arts Council and the Book Publishing Tax Credit.

Artwork created with graphite and finished digitally.

Author photo by CBC
Cover and interior artwork by Julie McLaughlin
Design by Rachel Page and Julie McLaughlin

ORCA BOOK PUBLISHERS
orcabook.com

Printed and bound in South Korea.

23 22 21 20 • 4 3 2 1

Johanna Wagstaffe is the meteorologist and science host for CBC Vancouver and CBC News Network. With a background in seismology, geophysics and earth science, Johanna has covered a wide range of science stories, including Hurricane Irma in Florida in 2017, the 2011 Japan earthquake and tsunami and the United Nations Climate Change Conference in Paris. The author of *Fault Lines: Understanding the Power of Earthquakes* and the host of the award-winning podcasts *Fault Lines* and *2050: Degrees of Change*, she enjoys sharing her passion for science education with children in schools and on social media. Johanna lives in Vancouver.

Julie McLaughlin is an award-winning illustrator whose work includes commissions for editorial, advertising and publishing clients from around the world. Her previous books have been nominated for several awards, including the Norma Fleck Award and Red Cedar Book Award for *The Art of the Possible*, and she won the 2015 Norma Fleck Award for Canadian Children's Nonfiction for *Why We Live Where We Live*. Julie grew up on the Prairies and now resides on Vancouver Island.